My
Worm Farm

Written by Mary-Anne Creasy
Photography by Michael Curtain

I have a worm farm. There are more
than two million worms on my farm.

I started the farm because
I wanted to get rid of garden rubbish.
I also care about the **environment**.

Worms can help us to get rid of our rubbish and to make **compost**. They eat food scraps, paper, and garden cuttings.

The worms' droppings are called **castings**. The castings make food for plants. I put the castings on the soil to help the plants grow better.

The worms at my worm farm are called **Compost Worms**. They eat anything **organic**, such as dead animals, leaves, and animal droppings. In the wild, these worms are found on the forest floor.

Compost Worms are not the same as the worms you see when you dig in your garden. The worms in your garden are called **Earth Workers**. These worms are gray and are much larger than Compost Worms.

Compost Worms   Earth Workers

Worms like to be kept warm and moist. They are kept in long raised beds with layers of coarse cloth and sacks on top. The cloth and sacks help to keep the **temperature** constant.

worm bed

coarse cloth   sack

There is a sheet of plastic
underneath each bed.
This helps to stop tree roots
from growing into the worm beds
and sucking up the moisture and
the **nutrients** the worms make.

plastic sheet under bed

plastic covering to keep
the worms warm in winter

Worms do not like light. At night they like to travel, so I put garden lights around the beds to stop them from getting out.

Worms do not like rain. They can drown in a heavy rain because they breathe through their skin. When it rains, worms will try to escape to higher ground.

Worms do not like to get too hot. In summer the worms must be kept moist. If the beds become too dry, the worms can die.

The worms feed on fruit and vegetables
that I get from the local market. I put the
fruit and vegetables into a machine that
mashes them. This makes them easy for
the worms to eat.

If there is too much fruit and vegetable
matter, the soil becomes **acidic**, or sour.
This isn't good for the worms. So I sprinkle
lime over the soil to help make it less acidic.

Worms can double their population every two months, so I never have to worry about running out of them. There can be as many as 12,000 worms per square yard (10,000 worms per square meter). Worms also travel from other places into the beds because there is plenty to eat.

egg

Worms lay eggs that are about the size of a match head. Up to ten young worms may hatch from each egg. However, in the winter, the breeding slows down. This means that fewer worms will hatch.

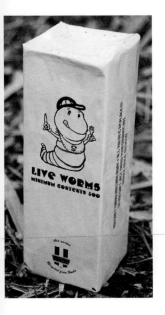

People come and buy worms for their compost piles and worm farms. They also buy worms to use as bait when they want to go fishing.

I can mail worms to people who can't come to the farm to buy them. I put some shredded newspaper in a box, and then I put in the worms. I put lots of holes in the box to let in air so the worms can breathe.

People can also buy small worm farms.
These are small compost bins with trays for
the worms to live in.

Glossary

acidic	sour; like acid
castings	worm droppings
compost	a mixture of rotting plant matter, animal droppings, and organic matter
Compost Worms	the type of worms that are used to make compost. They eat leftover fruit and vegetable matter.
Earth Workers	the type of worms that are found in a garden. They dig deep down into the earth. They feed on rotting plant and animal matter.
environment	the place in which we live
lime	a type of powder that is used on crops to make soil less acidic
nutrients	food
organic	living; something that was once living, such as a plant or an animal
temperature	how hot or cold something is